ONKONKAY

For Iris, Helen, Catherine, Matthew

Onkonkay

KEITH HOWDEN

HARRY CHAMBERS/PETERLOO POETS

First published in 1984
by Harry Chambers/Peterloo Poets
Treovis Farm Cottage, Upton Cross, Liskeard, Cornwall PL14 5BQ

ISBN 0 905291 44 1

Printed in Great Britain by
Latimer Trend & Company Ltd, Plymouth

ACKNOWLEDGEMENTS are due to the editors of the following journals, in whose pages some of these poems first appeared: *The Sunday Telegraph Magazine, Omens, Encounter, Bananas, Other Poetry, Midlands Worksheet, Poetry Review* (1978 Competition supplement).

Cover illustration: author's own montage incorporating 'Arrival of The Bear' by Oxley Grabham (1910) courtesy of The Royal Photographic Society.

SUBSIDISED BY THE
Arts Council
OF GREAT BRITAIN

Contents

Every year, the Onkonkay came heralded into the village by the song 'Ay addy Onkonkay'. The Onkonkay was a sacked figure trapped in a mesh of ribbons and might have been associated with fertility or even sacrifice. But it was a landscape of few long traditions, with its deepest roots in the industrial revolution, and 'Ay Addy Onkonkay' was only the voice's imitation of the trumpet call announcing a dancing bear.

Village

Under slack pylon cables, the road rears,
striking along the slope to spit
its gravel on the ravaged fell that wears
humpback the millstone terraces of spent

and broken village. My mother helplessly
wove her life's poverty in this mill shed;
her father quarried stone where pillage industry
blasted the hill, looting its bone to build

the warscape village. This tied house he paid
his health for in the ruin battery
of terraces that, stillborn and rape-child,
straddles its mother's hacked and swollen belly

since the hill workings failed. A millstone Chapel
pointed pathetic hope and reached to stone
but missed the sky. Here men chopping the fell
dug millstone pits to shape subsistence prison

and girls at looms wove ignorance to dress
their lives' dependence. And the siege surround
of moor won slow starvation; a relentless
rust at its kissing sabotage unmanned

the iron on the fell. The stealthy terrorists
of wind and frost sapped the mill wall. And here,
beleaguered at its barricade outposts,
the expedition failed. Now the wolf moor

licks at its wounds with clean and tissue greens
grassing to flesh the slowly healing scars
of rank allotments and deserted pens.
The landscape says, this stone was never yours;

in tumbled walls, hostage and held for fee,
it knows survival patience and will know
its womb again. It settles now to be
organic with itself, primal where you
were always strangers. This slow ferocity
of grass counter-attacking tells you so.

9

Onkonkay

Onkonkay
at the year's blasting
his horned statement
beware is coming.

Of the high fell
pelted like moorland
drinks at the black streams
under thunder feasts
bright berries
of mountain ash.

Spare on the black fell
rules the raped moor
scours the waste tarns
is thorns' king
the wind's lost beast
whose breath acid
whose language stone
stalks the sour marches
comes trumpeting
his beaked festival.

Moves now
his ponderous dance
on these pavements
comes yearly coiled
in children black strength
garlanded
in ribbons to drum
these mean streets.

Beware is coming.

2. ONKONKAY SHOUT

Am
anarchic
stinking sweet sack
Onkonkay
mischief's mechanic
ay
addy
Onkonkay
madness make mine.

Am
kissing's
kind kingdom come
Onkonkay
licence's lust lord
ay
addy
Onkonkay
musting make mine.

Am
disorder's
daft dancer dirty
Onkonkay
misrule's makar
ay
addy
Onkonkay
mending make mine.

Am
grace's
god goat garbled
Onkonkay
mademan manmade
ay
addy
Onkonkay
mystery make mine.

Am
sacrifice's
sinful sack slain
Onkonkay
sweet saviour
ay
amen
Onkonkay
mercy make mine.

3. ONKONKAY AMONG STONES

Comes at grass's
urgent call
is father of rocks
only begetter
of landscapes
comes now
to prance the balls'
religion the cods'
concertina among
these standing stones.

Sucks now at flesh's font
gropes the earth's pod
is brown rifle of
spring's green bullet.

Comes now at
these stones
this sack of sperm
battering his seed
to swell them
pregnant with pebbles.

Here rides
frantic with seed
pumps now his fecund sperm
to the land's belly
permeates
the cold cores of stones.

12

On this stone bed
bites back green life
in the husked seed
prints increase's impress
on rocks' membrane
in the nerves of pebbles
in sinews of stone
begets landscapes.

4. ONKONKAY FLAYED

O cruel boys
short trousered
spindleshanked
have killed
my Onkonkay
stripping his pelt
from a pale flesh.

A god dies here
lies now
an emptied sack
its beast dancing
done bright ribbons'
wounds untangled.

O cruel boys
have stripped
burl hide to bare
raw flesh beneath
out now
the naked twitching nerve
the bleb sinew
of this god's dance.

Peel his skin from him
his guts elastic
white as worms they
have hauled out of him.

Each year
is born is torn
ripped skin from flesh
this chrysalis god
now counts and gloats
pence at the roadside.

Is born is torn
from Onkonkay's wreck
O return to us
king of elders' froth
lord of haws' ferment
clown of streets' dance
when blunt earth
ploughs from this time
a year's space.

5. CHOOSING ONKONKAY

Who born is torn?
Who fool this year's fool
dancing daft
sacked in the streets?
Who garlanded goes
goating on grass?
Who ribboned rides
chariots of children?
Who hurrah is coming?
Who torn is born?

Who torn is born?
Who fool this year's god
rutting ripe
spawn among stones?
Who beaked batters balls'
religion rants
cods' concertina crowns
the groin's gantry?
Who hallows harrows?
Who torn is torn?

Who torn is torn?
Who god this year's god
hallelujahs
horned on the hill?
Who thorns' thane
is earl of elders'
ferment fine fashioner
of haws' hieroglyphic?
Who harrows hallows?
Who born is born?

Who born is born?
Who god this year's fool
comes ribbon-raped?
Who naked nerved his guts'
elastic white as worms
has hauled out of him?
Who dies pelt peeled
god garbled fool framed?
Who beware is coming?
Who born is torn?

Paradise Street

In eighteen thirty seven
under the shove of moor
whose lipping lodge
forever threatened
inundation, men started
here, Coronation
and Paradise Streets.
Canada revolted.

Under the millstone edge
they shaped twin thrusts
of civilisation's
lisping advance. Cotton
came and went; there was
the enduring stink
of steam while they
were building Paradise.

Chartists rioted.
The long chimney smoked.
While men were shaping
stone to assault
the moor's unready
hinterland, cold rain
persisted. There was
little prosperity.

When men were raising
Paradise, Victoria
pouted squat on the throne.
Looms clattered; slate
shone; Melbourne resigned.
In a wet summer came
the ragamuffin settlers
to stuff the mill's maw.

Newman sold out to Rome.
There was the first
site death and war
in Afghanistan while they
completed Paradise.
And not long afterwards
Peel's hand was forced
by famine in Ireland.

2. NEW DELIGHT

I Harold Ashworth's vision, 1820

That place I called New Delight,
our benign parish, our green
trust's parable, our sweet retreat.
Daily I kissed its earth's
abiding paradigm. Elsewhere,
maypoles were pricking Heaven's grandeur;
girls innocent in muslin white
tripped the sap's jubilee.
Gross festivals of lurching bears
ruled the moor villages; uncouth
and lumbering, were life's sumptuous
testimony to the breath's
benevolence. In our pure paddock,
we held no need for liquor more
than the sweet streams. It was
our grand intoxication; our lives'
great drunkenness; our new
delight. My spirit warbled
delight at New Delight.

II A Geography of Northern England, 1847

Sometimes the high moorland
falls steeply to secluded valleys.
The bleak heights are suddenly
transformed to succulent dells,
deep groves of fertile soil.
Nothing in these benign oases
speaks the sparse language
of the great fells. Remarkable

17

transitions, they afford
the diligent traveller new delight.
Simple communities, rude but gentle,
unused to strangers, offer
such hospitality as their
despite of alcohol allows.
In these secluded spots they lead
a coarse, devout existence,
holding in such precarious
circumstances, communality
of goods and life. . . .

III *A History of East Lancashire, 1892*

Small factional groups of these
dissenting religions raised
communes in the secluded valleys.
Abjuring alcohol, they lived
temperate lives. Independent
Methodists in particular formed
Chapels. Many used fields or hills
for their impassioned worship.
At best they had the use of farm
outbuildings. In barns and sheds
they preached a radical
sharing of goods and labour, a new
delight in the repudiation
of riches. Difficult transport
made their lives solitary and held
looseness in check. But such
guileless dependence failed.
These 'grand communities of God'
bred the dissent of men. . . .

IV *The Pennine Drinker, 1964*

Fearing the breathalyser,
circuitously by the moor roads
that stalk forgotten pack-horse trails,
we dropped to New Delight. The car
stuttered unwillingly at
the steep descent. Snow furred the fells.
In the deep valley, traceable,
dismembered outlines ate the snow
where the once village squatted.

Who built here? What wild community
of faith endured these unforgiving
uplands? Now only the one
structure remains, the lingering name
stuttering on broken slates.
Ghosts more than guests inhabit
the New Delight. Our sandwiches
were dry and curled; the beer
was barely drinkable; our host
surly and inhospitable. . . .

3. NAMING FARM, 1823: HUBERT ASHWORTH'S ACCOUNT

My father (a man much prone
to hearing voices) heard voices.
They told him where to build; told him
secrets for the construction
of an enduring shelter
in that cold riot. They told
dreams of fertility—a long
bristle of barley bearding
the waste moor; fat sheep. They spoke
a benign climate's imminence.

My first coming to that place
I shall not forget. Ewes and lambs
bawled behind me; the lame ram
Topaz belched ahead. Wind wheedled
ghosts' voices out of the rock.
Our black mule Benjamin lost
his nimbleness there. Another
delivery of voices told
what stone to use, what size a door;
where light should hole each wall.

That pleasant name, my father,
with a slim chisel, carved
in the lintel's stone. For years
we starved there. Lame Topaz died;
our sheep rotted. The moor
stayed sour. Those ghost voices whined
louder on each year's wind.

19

No barley crowded the waste slope.
Walls crumbled and my father's
voices crashed inside his head.

I said we built too high. His
voices spoke otherwise. The moor
was sour there, the starveling land
unredeemable. Stinking bogs
would rot the sheep and winters
starve us. My father (a man
much given to prodding awake
his sleeping voices) asked them
what was that place's name.
The voices said, 'Barley Top.'

4. TO SEE THE BEAR, 1829: JOHN ASHWORTH'S ACCOUNT

I

Mostly to see the bear, because
Tom Broadley and myself
had never seen one. Tom said
it would be freedom. That May day,
we climbed secret through fern,
ballocks of old sheepshit staining
our palms on the moor slope.

We went to see the bear. Under us,
our ranting creed's contraltos
hoisted in lambent light their
poisoned anthem; bass blew
impassioned along the valley's shed.
Tom shouted 'Hypocrites.' I followed
higher, towards our finer fervour –

to see the bear. I was fourteen.
Years older, Tom, not long before
a ranter himself, swore to me
our garden was already rotten,
our Eden apple mumbled
to its spit core. Our Eves, he said,
gasped open-thighed in bracken;

our Adams' arses nightly
bubbled white on the moor. Better,
Tom said, to see the bear.
Our 'grand community' was
a dafter time's delusion. Now he
cursed that lost dream of grace.
Better to see the bear.

II

Grouse clacked, 'Go back, go back.'
Larks raved in bright air.
We heard both. Curlew and cuckoo
were raucous round us. Bog-cotton
spangled the sour tops. We strutted
monarchs of the May's jubilee
on the moor's evangelism.

We danced to the moor head.
Under us, a sprained landscape
buckled. Long water in a canal's
incision filched the light. We were
spring's mandarins. It was
all ours, all sun. The warming soil
grew fertile under our feet.

We skirted quarries. A steep face,
stones shuttering from our boots,
dropped us towards the scrape
of village staining the slope. Clear air
raged round us. Then there came
the stench of steam; rust blooded
the torn earth. There was a Maypole.

III

Tom boozed in the Glory, staggered
drunk to the dancing. Our sun
deserted its blithe morning.
A few girls jigged through ribbons
to a punctured concertina.
Tom belched and swore. A trumpet's
addy onkonkay announced

the bear. To drums and pipes,
and somewhere a split tambourine,
the poor beast hauled from nature
gallumphed and lumbered, twitched to be
a silly toy. We came to see
the bear. It capered to
a cacophany, lurched a despite

of its divine invention. Foul
and shit-stained, shambled. Tom said—
To see the bear. Heaven's animal,
that beast of blood and growls
(so our book called it) slouched
to a banged tin's rhythm, pranced
humiliated in ribbons,

a muck dance to amuse and serve
a barren system. To see
the bear. Tom hiccupped. A blown
trumpet's onkonkay replied.
Children cheered. There was
cotton waste on the wind, a dog's—
coat stench of stagnant canal.

IV

Grouse clacked, 'Go back, go back.'
We heard them. Cuckoo and curlew
were quiet then. Tom vomited. We
slogged to the moorhead.
A fine rain corrupted the day;
cloud ate the village under us,
swallowed Maypole and bear.

Grouse clacked, 'Go back, go back.'
I heard, onkonkay. Tom said
it would be freedom. After that
sour Pentecost, I did not know
if we were free or not.
'Onkonkay' the insistent
grouse questioned. Those poor

syllables told me new truth.
Man's self of blood and growls
subdued to a ninny's toy.
Our lusting Adams butted
a purer air; our gasping Eves
jerked nearer grace than those
shawled starvelings. Our silly system

was lovelier than that barren
cavort in ribbons. I saw then
only the fettered limbs,
the mouth muzzled, the gived
gestures. Grouse clacked, 'Go back.'
I remembered the hostage
dancers and their muck jubilee.

5. DANCING BEAR

After the ribbons
and tambourines
he said
the booze and the bear
he said
we came to a barn.

After the dancing
drums and pipes
he said
the booze so drunk
he said
sneaked there to sleep.

After the boozy
kisses and gropes
he said
skirts slapping grass
he said
it was a shock.

After the bear's
gallumphing twisting
he said
(and once it shat)
he said
to find it there.

On the barn's straw
asleep like lovers
he said
man curled in bear
he said
for warmth it touched me.

6. DOHERTY COMES, 1839: GEORGE ASHWORTH'S ACCOUNT

I

Barley Top I was born, the waste
farm in the moor's waste. No
sustenance in that wuthering
windscape. The dry grasses
boiling in summer, the bracken
ablaze for autumn, stones
clattering in the ravines, snow
strangling its lost winters.
I curse that dream of barley.
Only the laming sheep; our walls
drawn by the earth's magnet; soil
acid and ungenerous. I knew
from birth that sour betrothal
of life to no just reward.

II

In a lean year's famine,
Sarah at my side, little James
in his box, I carried
to Paradise Street. We had known
snow late and early; lambs lost;
the blood blots staining snow of
our flock's miscarriages.

My father said God's hand
moves in disaster. What we knew
was clemmed bellies, the unfed
infant clamouring and succour
nowhere. In snow we dropped,
beggars, near Christmas, footsore,
to Paradise from Barley Top.

III

The torches I remember
and a new brotherhood in the wind
climbing the broken slopes.
Light's jumping geographies
roared new community. We served
a barren system; waste labour
and empty bellies again. This light
told grander visions, our torches
blades to a better life.
And climbing, hill beyond hill
in the stretching darkness
was scored with flame, our new
ignorant brotherhood flaring
new light, new hope, a new faith.

IV

Under cold Plough and frost stars,
a martial drum, a blown bugle's
addy-addy. We marched to
a Frenchman's song and followed
the man with the Irish name.
We had liberty on our tongues;
he shouted barricades. The wind
wore both impartially. We brayed
our dream to write our names,
to shape our letters, read.
A right to arm, he shouted. Wind's
charter battered, snuffing
our hopes' flames, whirring words
to gargles in the moor's anarchy.

V

I knew the seasons' pace, the days'
image that drove to empty
bellies. I know this nearer
harnessing to machines that drives
to empty bellies. I yearn sometimes
for the sweet winds and grasses
of the tops, for the sun's
inequalities of ground and sky.
This is a barren system.
Calamity from Heaven's fist I
endure; injustice from
man's hand I shall not brook.
Little James must read. This is
a barren system. It must fail.

7. DAMBREACH, 1871: JAMES ASHWORTH'S ACCOUNT

All summer it seemed to rain;
all summer we heard
the overflow's thunder
and belch, white water
cannoning against the sky.

The soughs were full, the groughs
sodden, the dykes and drains
never without a skin
of moving water. The turf
was sprung with rain; even
the stone tracks we laid
so carefully in former years,
even the flat, absorbent tops
were a knee's depth in slime.

All summer without naming it
we feared it. The air pulsed
with whatever it was.
In the mill pools, the goldfish
trembled afraid; the whole
tingling land seemed fixed
in an anxiety. We felt it.

The women drew their shawls
tighter; the children's games
ended sooner at night; men
whispered of coming trouble.
We did nothing. It was
no more than we were used to—
anxiety, the impending sense
of worse on the way.
But this was different.

II

All summer it rained;
all summer the white
overflow's cannon thundered;
all summer the soughs were full
and the whole land seemed
pulsing with hidden water.

The bank broke at night;
like other evils it used
darkness to shield itself.
We felt the tremulous
overtures, the sharp crack
of the very land that only
those who have heard it know.
It is the opening of a wound,
the tearing of a scab; it rips
suddenly. Those of us
who heard it know its name.

III

All summer the gurgle
of streams running beneath us
disturbed our sleep. All summer
the petty percolations
of soil from under us
troubled us. The sponge
of moor over our heads,
that impending sense
of worse on the way
was with us, different.

Mud squeezed between stones.
The buried stanchions of stone
deep in their earth bank
groaned and collapsed.
Stone shaped to lock its place
in the retaining wall
chattered and relaxed,
began its greased tumble,
towards us. A great wall
of water towered and fell.

IV

All summer the women
had drawn their shawls tighter.
We had whispered together
of impending trouble
and had done nothing.
Children whined in their sleep;
the dogs and cats deserted us
without warning. Even rats
in the gardens had gone.
All summer the overflow's
white cannon reverberated
under a rain-stacked sky.

Water broke among us,
tore stone from stone, gave us
no warning. We had had
only the rain's relentlessness;
only the whining and leaving
of our dogs; our children's
moaning in sleep; our women
quiet in their kitchens.
Stone bounced and broke
on stone; walls slipped; the world
seemed to collapse. There came
the land's breaking crack
that blasting storm of black
water roaring among us.

John Fagan they said, sailed
a mile and a half on
a table overturned; Alice
Webster crushed by her own stove;
George Broadley drowned; and two
were discovered naked
in the act of love, broken
by a falling chimney. God knows
how we go discovered
to what awaits us. Jane
Bradshaw was saved by prayer;
a tumbled joist trapped Henry
Parkinson. Some swam;
many were drowned.

V

All summer it seemed to rain.
All summer without naming it
we feared it. All summer
the soughs were full, the dykes
and drains never without
a skin of moving water.

I do not understand floods
or if some grand, assigned
meaning exists in torrents
or moves in cataracts.
Some saw God's purposes.
I see nothing. For me
there is no meaning in
the land's shattering, the water's
ungoverned ferment, the fall
of what men have laboured to build.
I ask only this—
what instinct do men lack
that the poor dogs and mice retain?
What have we forged ourselves
more important than that?
There is need now
to rebuild. We need help
and no-one aids us. We have
become hungry and share
what little we possess.

After the carnage, vultures,
after the carrion, crows.
The black hooded things dropped
early to suck our anguish.

Days after, we stood above
the broken bones of our homes,
the chattels of our poor lives,
their open wounds luring
such coward predators.

In the basin of the flood's void
fish flapped on caking ooze,
their flesh drying and stinking.
We feared disease. Green
fungus had stained their gills.
Not so the crows; thin feet
embroidered the mud's new nakedness.

And there were others.
A black sun burned behind him,
and under him our broken limbs
of hopes and homes, our sweet landscapes.
'Ye are a mayfly's dance.'
Wind twitched his predatory wings.
I saw then the mayfly tumble
of our white children's bodies
in the water's maelstrom;
the insect jerk of two-man stones
juggled in air like mating bugs
by the flood's force. That was
no dance for a dry moralist.

'Ye are a mayfly's dance.'
A cold wind flapped among
has blackened feathers. I saw
only the shards of our insect lives,
the chitinous bins that hold
whatever of us here is more
or less than flesh. Ours was
no dance for a hot evangelist
to point a rotten moral.

It is a blind and vicious will
that visits such destruction
on age and innocence. I shall
believe no more. Three of us threw
this squawking blood-bird
to the new filth below. Ours was
no dance to salt a ranter's belch.

9. CREDO, 1872: JAMES ASHWORTH

I

Bones bigger than men they bared,
quarrying raw moor to gouge
the earth with the lodge's wound.
My father's father saw it.
Gigantic thighs of creatures
unimaginable; ribs big
as the second limbs of elms;
teeth heavy as buckets; skulls
with sockets cavernous enough
for men to pass through.
Patrick Fagan told my father
the Irish hired to dig there
feared them as devil's work,
bones planted to confound us
and misguide our thought. At night
they broke them, in a riot smashed
those vault skulls to fragments.

II

Jane Bradshaw's child was born
with the head of a sheep and nascent
horns of a sheep; was hooved. I think
we start in the womb as fish,
swim there as fishes and come
in that jelly place to be
a spectrum of the beasts until
we breach as men. But bring
no more with us to air
than this poor ancestry. I think
there were giants once, and men
we would think monkeys.

I do not doubt that men
were simpler once, poor creatures
only of instinct. This
lurch offspring of Jane Bradshaw's
belly tells me as much.

III

I have seen men and stones
juggled in air like mating bugs
by the flood's torrent. Our dogs
and cats, poor beasts of instinct,
were three days fled. What nature
do they translate? What have men
bartered to pretend to this
perverse morality? There seems
wild wisdom in nature, but one
that cannot twist into a code's
disguised divinity. Nature's
force is destruction; nothing
in that long riot moves
to grace or goodness. My sky
speaks heaven's emptiness, the fells'
language is empty bellies
howling the moor's magnificence.

Barley Top

Came to the ruined dry-walled farm
in one of the barren folds of the hill,
its rafters raking the wind, its barn
vanished, and on the perching lintel, still

crudely but deeply chiselled was the name
I'd sought, the legend—Barley Top. It crooned
of my grandfather's boyhood, wasted time,
life undernourished on infertile ground.

Even now, though rushes and bog-tufts spread
and vaulted walls and dragged aside the door,
a different, limier green betrayed
land lost to and recaptured by the moor.

I thought of those old builders, the sour land
desolate, unpropitious to their hope;
the name declared their optimism, and
sheep they must have kept, but Barley Top

spoke languages of pathos, the frail nimbus
of stillborn dream, and Barley Top broken,
crumbling at the moor's relentlessness,
was every foundered prospect for me then.

Wind trapped and blundering among the stones
took me to times that solitary, wry,
my grandfather acknowledged as his own,
shoeless before the turning century.

Picture of Lil

This sepia portrait bit brown air when card
was card and Heaven's tenant listened. Lil's
cobbled road is clear. She stands outside
her father's shop among the etched cathedrals

of letters arched on glass behind her head:
'Fine Fruit and Vegetables', where, inside
the shop, a sepia season's fruit is piled,
and the late century's tomato trade

pouts on display. Street side of glass, the spread
of fruit is not so fine. My cousin Lil
swelled only half-wit in a bunch that made
much point of speculating why. That smile

carved on her rind is fixed; its wrinklings chart
unsucculence in poor and withered fruit.
Her sole fertility, that marvel of a wart,
sprouts on her nose end. Spindly at its root,

it plumps, a pregnant exclamation mark,
prodigious, like a damson on her face.
When wartime trapped us in the black-out dark
famine of moors, it brought evacuees

who saw her with new eyes and itched to poke
such oddity. Through their clear eyes I saw
past custom's blindness. Lil was a cruel joke.
Let savages hold the idiot in awe;

Lil's mother specialised in supplications,
publicly asking what Almighty Will
in Heaven's tenant posted such simpletons
to plague His world. I rumbled Cousin Lil

was daft as life itself and speculation on her
pointless where lack of clothes conceals no emperor's
presence. Such famine fruit I learned to gather
at wartime games on the agnostic moors.

Uncle Tom and Auntie Lizzie

Uncle Tom taught me algebra; his math-
ematics had A always as one, B two.
I never solved equations. He hit me with
his walking-stick so hard it fixed a blue

weal on my bum. My Uncle Tom taught me
the language of flowers, a daftness I
quickly forgot. Tom had seen angels fly
across the sunset. In the framed *Agony*

of Faustus on his wall, he used to see,
if it were damp and only he were there,
the Devil's face. My mad and shouting Auntie
Lizzie complained of deafness to her Doctor

who told her, at her loom for thirty years,
she had lip-read for ten. His diagnosis
brought her a pair of spectacles as ears,
whose sharpness told her the unkind asides

the cameras caught at royal weddings. Then
I made a buzzer that could simulate
the noise her deaf-aid made when it was on
the blink. And though the thing was working right,

that shrieking buzz convinced her it was broken.
She threw it on the fire. After that, she could
be fooled by mouthing noises, lip-reading when
nothing was spoken. Now both of them are dead.

I pray some region of the spirit's reach
for Uncle Tom, where A is one, B two;
valhallas of such errant logic; such
landscapes as he would want where flowers grow

articulate. My mad Aunt Lizzie fitted
her end to that most subtle irony
in which the finely-tuned machine transmitted
the image of its fault so perfectly

it finished in the fire. A sphere so crude
needs little search. I pray her better luck
next time. For her at least death came unheard.
I hope Tom got him with his walking-stick.

Ringworm

Earth's baldest fairies marshall a white line
for wartime concert. Played false by the malign
    spirit of things, they posture in
    a never-never land of pantomime;
    for this is nineteen thirty-nine—
    the year the girls got ringworm.

Where are you now, coy bullet-heads,
    Jean, Margaret, Mary, Joan?
Plain names, plain girls to match
    (now nearing fifty)
    where have you all gone?

Potato heads protrude from tulle. This is
their minute of bashed vanity. Here they lose
    faith in a child's world's comely ways,
    grasp a new truth of living's pantomime.
    Blotched gentian violet betrays
    the year they all got ringworm.

Where are you now, bald-headed girls,
    Jean, Margaret, Mary, Joan?
    Plain names, plain minds to match
    (now forty years adrift)
    What have you thought and done?

Collaborator heads parading here
can hardly treasure this wartime souvenir.
    Girls shaven and crestfallen
    stare, novices, into life's pantomime;
    for this is nineteen thirty-nine.
    More than the girls got ringworm.

Where are you now, lost ringworm girls,
    Jean, Margaret, Mary, Joan?
    Plain names, plain fates to match,
    bald from that past you shine
    fixing some ringworm mine.

Cracked Mary

1. CRACKED MARY'S MILL

I

They call me mad. My father's,
his father's father's mill this was.
Now mine. Brick broken fingers
crude for the sky's soft pieces.

I watch through dolly-blue, false
curtains of my window glass's stain,
cavorting children dance the walls.
Weeds reach to trip. I laugh in noon

green to the sun, stalk ruinous
garden's tangle, my father's
paths, my mother's luminous
borders blown. Convolvulus

is snakes; stiff parasol cow-
parsley cracks; elderberries
flutter my hand's rape. Now,
among the mossed Morrises

(dead Papa's cars) and fungus
(dear Mama's) Fords, I twine green
by the burst walls' bellies.
Was once their mill. Now is mine.

II

Copperplate, indentured,
forty apprentice orphans
fevered within a week. Rye bread
so black and soft it clung the gums

like putty; sometimes porridge
sour and blue, their foul diet.
Poor starvelings, before that rage
pestilence, death's appetite,

fell at their looms; vomited
life on the cloth; were maimed by
senseless machines; screaming died;
saw horrid visions. Secretly

at night, my father's father,
his father fired to cleanse the stall,
pitch and tobacco to deter
the fever's rampage; had girls sprinkle

vinegar to cure the beds
of retching children. So much death,
rumour swears their shallow sheds
unconsecrated heave beneath

Fords and mossed Morrises
of this tumultuous soil.
Some say their bones crack in these
blanched towers of weed, straddle

their flesh through elders, bulge in
fat palms of hut-high nettles
as another century's pain
whose squalour forces the rank grass.

III

I am the white flower's dance
in the night garden, twisting,
am moth and phosphoresence.
Am maiden silk trysting

with ghosts. Am seven veils bare.
My midnight garden riots
pregnant with phantoms. They are
here, those fevered unfortunates.

Fat worms have awled them; the gleam
belly of lodge butting the weir
quivers old anguish. I am
the cupped convolvulus flower.

In the stilled wheel's genital
their screaming. My midnights' breed
cold flames in the crumbled wall.
I am the white petal freed.

More than the mousing cats, these
shadows cluster. One of them
loves me. His name is Peerless.
Among mossed Morrises, in drum

landscapes we lie. He touches
me strangely. Oh then the fine
champagnes of my body! Peerless
speaks secretly his passion.

I am my mill's Salome
at midnight nautches where,
damaged and exultant, I
dance the cracked flesh's grandeur.

2. CRACKED MARY SEES THE PHOENIX

Feral doves float the rickety
mill shed; among the stilled looms'
corroding limbs, cruise perfectly
the alleys between. No-one comes.

Nothing turns here. Now there are
no clogged girls cancelling silence.
Feral doves colonise rafter
and belt in the roof's decadence,

clatter the unmuscled air
of bobbin corridors. They squeeze
filth through the rot gossamer
mantling the shuttles' disease.

One built low. To form her haunt,
filched metal fins from the warp-combs,
mimicing straw. At light's urgent
command, went stripping looms

to build an iron nest. Spring forged
a sole squab in that mesh—bulge pelf
cheese bellied, milk-cloud eyed
whose bill agape raged self

and shrieked survival's greed.
That was no fledgeling. Phoenixes
or basilisks roar that creed
from shrapnel nests in iron trees.

Feral doves float the stilled looms'
corrosions; unmuscled seasons
flutter the shed. Only rust blossoms
iron copses. No phoenix happens.

I

That summer, the wrecked *Foudroyant*
whaled on the beach, her rig awry,
her terraces of cannon cant,
I feared, to blast my holiday

God out of his sky. That summer,
under a shrieking seagull,
Mama's heels pecked the wet bladder
of strand. There was the rank smell

of donkeys and hot sand. Papa's
boozed baritone hurled '*What are
the wild waves saying?*' at the sea's
equal intemperance. Later,

in a shell's telephone, I
begged to be loved. Another
seagull dropped shrieking; a donkey
hee-hawed. The sea said, None to spare.

42

II

That summer I learned to fly;
rode the *Big Wheel* to value
a doll world under me.
Mama was the black sequin who

waved upwards, Papa the tipsy
tiddleywink. The greenhouse *Winter*
Gardens flashed sun. Epilepsy
twisted the world miniature.

Suspended, I learned love's posture.
Harsh kiss and impassioned hand
in the compartment corner
ignored a child. All they attained—

passion's squeals and grunts—I made mine.
I ached to be loved. The wheel
wound landscapes up and down.
Level gulls roared, Not possible.

III

That summer, the sham pavilions
on the pier's plank spewed flesh. So much
sweat and breath, like Resurrection's
pale millions blinking their retch

from earth. So much snot and skin,
a maggots' dance, the mills' pupae
unearthed and wriggling in the sun.
Mama pouted headache: Papa

snored gin to his afternoon's
boredom. A few gulls shrieked for
gobbets. I posted sixpence
through boards to the sand under.

Eye to that slit, I watched them:
sprawled gropers in the pier's shadow.
I yearned for love, but lust's drum
under me said, Not here, not now.

44

IV

That summer, to the Tower's
Longstone, I played Grace Darling;
at a polished sea, bucked her water's
rodeo. An epsom salting

at the tide's crawl rim was my
lashed Farne. One gull's syllable
pumped a petrel and fulmar sky.
Mama, I thought, too stoical

at her rescue. Dear Papa
hiccuped at the benign swell,
tossed guts in a bored parabola
to that poised, hammering gull.

Papa bubbled vomit. A steamer
hooted. I craved love. A few
fish threshed in a box. Mama
said, Not for me, never for you.

45

V

That summer, Mama said No.
I, at Papa's insistence,
was hauled through new Meccano
lattices to the Tower's glans.

Sea had more weft than warp from there.
We gloated the diminished
and futile world together.
Then Papa jumped. I heard

his last hoot and saw him leave,
seagull spreadeagled in his last
drunkenness. He seemed to wave
goodbye. I had no tears. The rest

is newspapers' babel. They
dropped me between Meccano.
I dreamed of love. Reality
screaming the ground said No.

46

The Fun

Blackpool in nineteen thirty-seven. This
devoted couple tread the boards and pull
daft faces at the man fixing their bliss
on Central Pier. Behind them, the sea wall

plays clap-hands with the sea. Victorian
ironwork rusts. The Tower's pear-drop head
points nothing. I am a child walking between.
Fred wears a suit and walks flat-footed

under a plate-size cap. He smiles. She has
white stockings and a wind-swirled skirt, a stout
and happy woman on her holidays.
This childless pair were gentle to my youth.

After she died, when she no longer sat
mammoth across his hearth, while his forgotten
fag-ends were cratering the leatherette
arms of his chair, he would be earnest in

fond conversation with her undepressed
cushions, reciprocal enough. For years
I never saw him. Then, when he was stretched
the pruneskin skeleton of that masher's

holiday smile, with spittle on his chin
and barely raising blankets on his bed—
'Me, you and Annie on the pier. The fun—'
he said, thought me a child again. He died

that night, as though I'd brought him home some stray
piece of himself, as though he held again,
to die complete, that day's entirety—
the child, the smiling man, the laughing woman.

Fell Street

1.

Promising somewhere else, it hymns
release from the prison pews
of lower streets and Chapel
bucking the landscape's truth.

It leans a Jacob's ladder
to scale the fell. On it,
tankers, fonts sour with acid,
lorries altared with cloth

mouth industry's matins,
haul out of this lay shadow,
strain to a higher crossing.
There, the stretched prospect

assembles new priorities
where an agnostic geography
maps the bewildered landscape,
promising nowhere else.

2.

Listen: a whining gear
of choirboys. Now bulge banners
wrestle where infidel wind
shudders the flexible

architectures of Zion.
Listen: the stalling engine
of piety's hired band
on these sceptical contours.

Now trumpets squeal their brakes.
Listen: a sermon's klaxon
batters the crossing. Broken verbs
bleat unaccepted over

grass's enduring atheism.
Observe: the summit breeds occasion
to map faith in a hurt landscape,
promising somewhere else.

3.

Promising nowhere else, Fell Street
wears pageants of narrow life.
Christ gored and bloody takes
his bump, annual ride. The tankers'

daily religion corrodes.
The land's skin is chastened
by acid. The moor's starved body
is yearly burned. The fell's limbs

are flayed by quarrying.
Canals incise. The road's census
tells only its traffic's hopes,
promising somewhere else.

Football Team

'They tell you your kind,' he said,
'that losing lot,' and pointed
the useless sides, immortal
under blurred glass, whose aspects
—petrified, agonistic—
spoke the language of my kind.
Photographs commemorate

the losing teams, winters in
the depressed thirties. There is
no crowd; imagination
must populate cloth-cap
brigades trapped tight for release.
The losing eyes stare and I
remember my kind. These played

to groans and roars. Not such men
as wanted neat applause or
recognition of finesse.
These ran, the carpenters of
ball-play, not its cabinet-
makers. I have known their kind.
Men trapped in caste and time by

grease licked hair, by posture, by
bull-necks shaved convict high.
They wear the insignia
of what they were—workaday
pros, not moneyed amateurs;
at it for cash. Combatants
in the lower leagues, the shabby

infantry, not the Lancers.
I know their kind. Fixed here by
time and class, small-time, small-hope
proletarian heroes.
I shall remember their sad
permanence of posture. It
tells me the language of my kind.

Eden Street

Eden Street's millstone funnel
proposed life's limited perspectives.
In seams of blackened stone and in
right-angle raids on cramped horizons

it wrote the bleak calculus
of our caste language. The wet planes
of Monday's drying sheets ordained
my class mathematics. Rockets

marking Novembers' red festivals
spumed straight down Eden Street;
Christmas's cold carols shot
resonant along its barrel. In frost

winters, a clog's spark at its end
was a new star glimpsed suddenly
through a Woolworth's telescope.
In Eden Street's millstone tunnel,

some cold October burgeons
this logarithm of love's experience.
A streetlamp's pinchbeck wounds
her tender surfaces, burns on

the bared stick of her wrist. Here lust's
algebra gilds its street Adam
luminous for his lost myth—
earth's first erotic flesh.

Castle Street

We mourned a death. Together we
remembered Castle Street.
For years we lived with hens on
Castle Street and never knew
its castle; squandered our wit
scratching for ruined Disney.
One sign of fastness, a piece

of tower, a battlement,
a bit of Lancelot would
have done. All that we got was
hens. Photographs from that time
conjure gaunt cats on walls; pole
starvelings under Bradman caps;
a square and stone-block Chapel.

Always brown hens. We woke to
the ratchet of chickens in
mill-morning pens, groping in
Castle Street for years without
guessing its castle. A slice
of helmet, a portcullis
would have done. Photographs breed

a scruffy heredity
of doormat dogs; a wartime
football nourished under clogs.
Brown hens. We never knew that
castle where archeologists
infer in broken ridges
and battered ground such proof as

scholars require for castles.
We wanted more. Photographs
propose life's monochrome; don't
predict these skull-eyed terraces
shattered where, in lost courtways,
strutting a slumping earthwork,
brown hens deride history.

Sulphur

Sulphur was my youth's cousin.
I suffered it my morning
bedfellow. It rode on air,
its yellow kinship mapping

that small world's geographies.
Sulphur was my youth's habit.
I knew its stink on workmen
home from the yards; and sulphur—

piles ornate as churches
pointed life's poor direction.
Sulphur was my youth's legend.
My Uncle shovelled sulphur

all his life, and my gross Aunt
who never loved him much,
swore on the night he died, she
watched the blue burn of his soul

in transit through her kitchen,
felt the oppression of
a brimstone air pinning her down,
heard, without seeing, his door

at an uncanny opening
and questioned if it were
him going or the Devil,
sulphurous, coming for him.

Stone Street

Succours no legend;
its language is itself.
Hangs over these
disordered cobbles
the sour taint of sulphur
blown from the yards.

Do not look here
for the rich lodes
of an engraved past.
Spawn the damp air
only the soft spasms
of steam and cotton.

No saga contends
fulfilment here.
Stone's parables point
nothing. It wears
no memory longer
than yesterday's fag.

Expect no history.
The waste villages
crapping the black slopes
know none. Here is
no enduring myth
of anything better.

No fable's franchise
traipses this windy
outpost of street.
Only the temporary
balladry of cash
wrangles in thin air.

Accepts no legends,
itself its own language.
No annals survive
of richer or greener;
and stone blockades
profounder expectation.

Chapel

They had square minds, these Chapel
builders; square blocks shaping square
precipice walls; square windows
whose mullions stand rock-solid for

this pennine gothic. Peter
built on a rock; here Wesleyan
apprentices, serving their time
ordained worship within one.

This was a square hallelujah shout
to ratch the fell's horizon
and to confound the sky's near circle;
a bawled non-conformist Amen.

Too square for a psalm's Hebrew curve,
it flings a dissenting hymn's
harmonium blast, industrial
and smoke blackened, that proclaims

God's millstone Mechanic's Institute;
a sermon factory for the crude
and rougher artisans of praise.
Here, eternity's indentured

millwrights tend the sturdy, square
machineries of salvation. Here,
within the rusty railing, white
marriages blaze on a redeeming stair;

black deaths drop out of temperance
to a long fermentation. Here
youth's randy pastimes bend
shadows from Chapel founders' square.

Canal Street

Crapped on the canal side, siezed
in a stiff genuflexion, Canal Street
told a cracked rosary of lodgings where
waste navvies of the cut's incision

decamped and spawned. Accents and names
still thick with Ireland, its slick
Sunday battalions, swallowers
of real flesh, living blood tramped

the moor to Mass. For us, the fell's
confining geographies, the moor's
scratch tilth, the bald landscape's
protestant intolerance wore God's

undoubted signature. Nothing within
heaven's predestined narrowness
subscribed Canal Street's easy religion.
What truth had ever flourished

under vines and sunshine? What business
had such passions of blood and tears
with the cold ethic of self-denial
our landscape sustained? What use

such technicolour transubstantiations
in our lives' monochrome contour?
We heard their mumbled mysteries; heard
their shocking supplications; watched

bloodstained and agonised, their Christ
of nails and sorrows, still convinced
that two crossed sticks raised in
our arid upland told profounder truths.

Canal

Leeds–Liverpool
canal
is Catholic.
Is rich in
water's rituals;
practises
no contraception;
accepts
flesh and blood.

Leeds–Liverpool
canal
is Methodist.
Pragmatic;
abhors pomp;
attempts
a workday ethic.
Fallen into
is not much fun.

Leeds–Liverpool
canal
is Anglican.
Money talks;
swings both ways;
owned by
the land
conforms to
the land's contour.

Leeds–Liverpool
canal
is agnostic.
Knows nothing
except questions;
runs from
beginning to end
making no guess
which is which.

Leeds–Liverpool
canal
is atheist.
Admits the
confinement
of its known banks;
trades with
no port beyond
its terminus.

Engineer, 1801

I

To navigate these hills! To bring,
traversing these uplands,
where nature itself could not,
our blunt barges! I have learned
this stubborn landscape; hard rock
and harder labour. Something
inimical inhabits these
squeezed geographies. These bald
protestant landscapes frighten
our Irishmen. They say there is,
in this miserable tilth,
some unforgiving spirit. We
have laid spades on it, have heard
it drumming under us, keening
beside us. The bog-men call it
Greenteeth. It haunts the wind's
screeching, has lodging in this
persistent rain from leaking skies.
Our tunnels are gouged; embankments
straddle the valleys; the long summit
nears completion. Soon, water
will bristle these uplands with
the reality Whitworth dreamed.

II

The mules and donkeys know it,
belching bloated on bitter grass.
Greenteeth, the Irish blame. We were
slicing that swathe, that cantle
from a land ungenerous
except with stone. Our days and nights
were cold. Barren days of rain
slowed us; wind clutched and strangled
the sour valley's throat. Our Irish
were unwilling and drunk.
Cassidy and Fagan decamped;
Mangan shrieked for priests where none

were findable; Durkin howled
for drink; others staggered drunk.
Cullen died screaming. Our bog-
navigators fought among themselves.
Greenteeth, they blamed. They claimed
the landscape haunted them; the bare
and unproductive moors made them
fearful. The gangs complained
of ghosts. Wind here plays tricks
among the rock slopes; wild water
runs underground groaning. This is
an unhappy landscape, torn
and battered by men before
our buffeting. Greenteeth
the gangs blame. Our Irish
are different; they see and hear
differently, respond sometimes
with the sharpened sense of animals
and share their fear. This landscape
is damned. Greenteeth, they call it.
The natives, now they know
the name of that fear, shout it
towards us. They hate us. The names
they have given to places
are sometimes gentle, but
this whole landscape raves revenge.

III

Greenteeth. The natives know it,
peering at us from ravines.
They come from and turn back to be
rocks of their habitation; come
and go without acknowledgement,
are heads seen momentarily
over the bluffs, stones shuttering
and no-one visible. They seem
miserable men, much given
to ranting, cursing the Pope
and drink; men easily given
to the spirit's movement.

It rises quickly in them. We hear
cold Hallelujahs clattering
from Chapels perched, clinging
to lowering hills, crude huts
of stone under parent stone.
In such tabernacles they rave
their landscape's long bitterness.

Jack Denison

1. DENISON DEAD

'Jack Denison,' he said. Near closing time
we climbed into the fell, where the land creases
and sours under the moor. Marching heat-hazes
    spun on the asphalt distances;
    pale sheep outcropping
were boulders on the slopes. Sun burned the calm.
'Denison' said the sunshine we were stepping.

Streams had burned dry. 'Jack Denison,' he said.
The worked-out drift lay sullen under us;
its iron guts bled rust on the poor pastures;
    the fan ripped from its innards was
    a rammel palace now
for heat-dazed sheep. Roof and walls had decayed.
'Denison' said the torn fan's tumbled shadow.

We turned down to the drift. The moor waited;
the hill was bare and harsh in the sun's blare.
Town's petty straggle trailed the valley floor
    with stagnant yards, Our Lady's spire.
    Sheep did not move
at our approach. 'Jack Denison,' he said.
'Denison' said the sun's long blare above.

'Jack Denison,' he said. His shoulder burst the lock
through its punk housing. I was afraid.
This was an eerie sepulchre of dead
    machines. Oil and thick grime encrusted
    blurred window-panes.
Dust spurted through the stained sunlight we broke.
'Denison' said the stench of dead machines.

In the drift's dusk, only that latent question
lived for us then. The blank machines were sullenly
hostile. In one of the grimed bench drawers, he
    reached for the torn Directory
    and shuddered from it
that unread message—'Tell Jack Denison—'
'Denison' said the brown and thumb-stained note.

'Jack Denison,' he said; the note's insistence
sucked the room's air to a foul prisoning,
swelled in its sound of sun-trapped flies with something
    oppressive in their heightened buzzing.
    The door seemed a release.
Outside, clean sunlight streamed, heat garbled distance.
'Denison' said the boom of clustered flies.

'Jack Denison,' he said. In a charged air,
the black flies fizzed, butting at dusty light
in the bleared windows. Then he tore the note,
    scraped it to secret in the grit.
    'I'm glad it's over.'
Either the buzzing ceased or ceased to matter.
'Denison' said the torn and shredded paper.

'Let him lie comfortable.' We went outside.
His hand swept over the spoiled valley floor,
and, far below, Our Lady's pricking spire.
    White pigeons in a flicker
    circled the sun.
It was all sun. 'Jack Denison,' he said.
'Denison' said the moor and straggled town

2. WHAT ARTHUR SAID

A bright day. Arthur said, 'Down on the floor
I saw his bloody hands.' Morning sun suckled
at chimney tits, drained a limp Guinness poster.
Bunched fists of cloud lay on the fell's long counter.
'Two hands and nobody with them,' Arthur said.

Blown dandelions were spurting filament
parachutes, seeding the river's barren pasture.
A woman in a mustard-coloured coat
dragged her snot child through sun in the back street.
'Whose hands?' I'd always known whose hands they were.

'No accident,' Arthur said. Pale sunshine knifed.
In the allotment, an old man's stoop attends
a sprawled dog with a bleeding foot beside
a broken frame. 'Jack Denison,' Arthur said,
carving the sunshine's trivial accidents.

'I didn't stir a limb,' he said. A young cat preened
on the yard wall, cocking a Dietrich leg
suspenderless behind her ear, and showed
a patchy undergut. Her pink teats plumped
pregnant to her coarse tongue's assuage.

'Struggling in the dark.' Across the pen,
girls in bright dresses flickered and the paling
danced summer's dioramas. The globe sun
bubbled bright gold. 'All the time struggling in
the bloody dark.' Our Lady's spire pricked nothing.

Children were plunging gravel at wet mud.
'Something you don't forget.' Boys balanced upright
on spoke-starved bicycles, their thin arms folded
to a proud handlessness. Sharp starlings banged
from roof to roof. Some things you don't forget.

3. ALLOTMENT

It is my mind's country, that dog-coat smell
of stagnant water scummed and pooled beneath
a sky domed and oppressive as a skull;
kaleidoscope allotments jaundiced with

the year's decay. Ripe elderberries blood
the bankside pens. Swifts at their gathering business
cleave the far hill; grey, captive cloud
clings like sheep's wool to wire on the fell screes,

teases to thinness, tears away. And thunder
mutters. Time-lapsed, another lightning stroke
shivers the water's plunge. Our Lady's spire
pricks nothing. The greenhouse windows shake

timpani to the thunder's bass. A sough
of shifting pressures swells the pregnant trees.
Loose felting slaps tattoos in alleys of
allotment huts. Wind moves in leaning marches

through the long bankside grass, draws swallows on
the water's pooling crust. It is my heart's
landscape. I see the eternal fashion
of bins and kennels in the stagnant yards;

thin runes of aeriels in the grey sky-fall;
the red bus on the hanging hill road; swifts
gathering degenerate. These are all
changeless. In clock-ring patterns, tethered goats

champ the unyielding twitch. In the playground,
swings creak. And there, among the broken rods
of sunflowers, the middle shift compound
their garden platitudes. It is my blood's

country. In buttress terraces that screw
the river's turn, cheap runners on brass rails
swing the spent green of curtains soughing to
the suck and pull wind's pressure at the sill's

slit ventilation. White and ignorant
of the blear spittle spark of thunder sun,
Jack Denison lies handless, buffets at
his bedclothes like a netted penguin.

He Tells His Love's Landscapes

Here swill my heart's landscapes:
clock dandelions spit their filament
symphonies in the yards; swifts cleave the hill.
Cloud on the counter fell
plunges; loose felting's soft timpani slaps
the long allotment's autumn music; wasps
forage and squander in the compost's rot.
Sharp starling regiments rout fallen fruit.

Here sprout my blood's boroughs:
grass seed in barren constellations sows
the river's restless firmament. Here stone
terraces plant my passion.
The red bus on the hanging hill road furrows
my bones' infertile pasture. Black water mirrors
a bulb's pale onion. A smashed stool wallows.
The cinder yards spawn brawling sparrows.

Here blister my skin's passions:
felled hay in hill fields pastures her flesh's cry.
At the high lodgeside, the disembowelled land
bares itself, arches its wound
of unhealed outcrop. The steep overflow shrines
cascading water. Under its bastions
ravished, bemused, beneath its tower we lay.
Swifts high and screaming pierce a bridal sky.

Here spits my seed's process:
the mountain ash spill blood along the fell.
Freed water thunders over the lodge's lip.
It was our Eden then, that deep
midgeridden gloom; that pooled sky; that rich sluice
bursting its business through the simple grass
of that deep hollow's wound; the green valley's fall.
The white boat bearing me is a murdered gull.

Here wasps my wound's legend:
sunflowers' broken rods drip shrivelled grain.
She bred me spring and fall, my mallard pleasure,
my autumn's flesh, my year
with its fat bellyfull. She swelled my knackered land
of goats tethered on twitch, my hands' playground
of summer's squealing swings; my barren garden.
Scrag bantams rut that parish's lost Eden.

Here stings my truth's ruin:
chrysanthemum heads are frosted hard as moons
in the midnight allotment. There has been
falling and budding since. Once mine
the clattering clockwork of the arched heaven;
was once a god; once tore time's tawdry curtain.
Here rips my silly minute's flail and dance.
Bursting my planet, here come the filthy swans.

Your Honour, Jack Barlow

I FROGSPAWN

I was lusting only for frogspawn there, Your Honour.
Still ponds were all I sought. This was in Eden
on its first apple day. Bluebells I think
were on the rampage; birds bustled in the banner
of rainbow light. The spring pools were green
with hanging trees and downward grasses sunk
in mirror parishes better than ours, Your Honour.

In Eden, threshing among green fern, Your Honour,
bashing among the bluebells, they were at it together,
that nearly naked possing on rainbow ground.
I watched them play young flesh's concertina
in a parish of butterflies. While I was there,
Adam gave Eve his gift of frogspawn and
regretted nothing. We call it love, Your Honour.

I was fishing only for roach that day, Your Honour.
They bite well on warm evenings. This was in Eden,
that late, corrupted summer. Hayfields, I think,
spilt their milk ointment on the wind. Could there
have been an untimely cuckoo? Every reflection
told mirror parables of a perfection sunk
and lost beneath the rainbow scum, Your Honour.

On the long bankside, where the canal, Your Honour,
breeds rainbow grasses and swifts dip, feasting in air,
I watched them quarrelling while the swans thrust near.
It was his frogspawn lodging squamous within her
that she complained of. This Eden day there were
no butterflies. The canal was a broken mirror
reflecting nothing. We call it love, Your Honour.

Your Honour, tell me the voices exist.
I hear them. I have always heard them. I
once thought myself the budding poet of
the twentieth century. I would have written
my landscapes rich and fortunate with apples
but the voices wavered and broke. I would
have written apples but the word came serpent.

Your Honour, I thought dead Abel's voice;
some have his accent. But there are others. I
thought I had poems to drive the world mad.
I would have written my landscapes nourishing roses
but the crippled rows straddling this unwelcoming
upland howled different voices. I would
have written roses but the word came thistles.

Your Honour, I thought your voice;
but you are voiceless, have never spoken. I
had wanted to write the kingfisher parishes
and friendship's inns. I would have written landscapes
favouring rainbows, but the bald fells
baying the rain's ache crippled my voices. I would
have written rainbows, but the word came sorrows.

Your Honour, whose voice speaks through us?
Coiled pipes and tripes is all we seem. I would
have written the world awake; I would have written
my landscapes succouring butterflies, but the blood's
insistence tainted such voices. I would have written
butterflies, but hear, coiled pipes and tripes
is all we are. Your Honour, are the voices real?

High Moor

Familiar landscape: the embattled road
beleaguered on the fell, climbing in coils
to the emplacement barns at broken guard
on the moor's famine marches. Bucking walls—

dry breastworks of attrition frontiers—
straddle the hostile ridges. A spiked wire
arches to shield the sour, decrepit pastures,
barbs the disputed border with the moor.

Bleak mile-post farms keep grudging sentry, sit
in camouflage, observing wearily
from limed and levelled fields, the torn retreat
of civil cultures in a territory

where moats of marsh and wheelsink wastes concede
moor mobilising and the massing squads
of ling and gorse. Larks' bursting enfilade
rifles each sector, and in caltrop fields

rushes are marshalled for guerilla war.
This land was never yours. No truce will quell
the propaganda rumble of the moor
relentlessly at broadcast; every subtle

fraternisation is a treachery.
The token force is weakened by erosion.
Attrition struggle favours those who lie
thickest and know the landscape. Occupation—

fortification and an alien culture
rudely enforced—will not outlast this slow
rebellion resentment. And you are
foreigners here—the lark's bullet says so.